Original title:
Buttons and Beliefs

Copyright © 2025 Creative Arts Management OÜ
All rights reserved.

Author: Atticus Thornton
ISBN HARDBACK: 978-1-80586-077-8
ISBN PAPERBACK: 978-1-80586-549-0

The Latch of Logic

In a world where quirks abound,
I tried to fasten reason down.
But every time I gave a pull,
It laughed and danced, my brain was full.

A sock refused to pair with me,
It claimed it valued liberty.
While spoons debated which one's best,
They stirred the pot, quite unimpressed.

The cat wore glasses, thought it wise,
To read the world through narrowed eyes.
Yet when it saw a butterfly,
It leapt and missed, oh my, oh my!

So here I sit, a curious chap,
With wiggly worms in my thinking cap.
Each thought like sprinkles on a cake,
I giggle softly with each mistake.

The Tapestry of Acceptance

In a field of mismatched shoes,
The left one's happy, the right one snoozes.
They weave a story, thread by thread,
Of all the places they would tread.

A pineapple wore a tiny hat,
Confident and quite the chat.
While lime gave sass, a zesty show,
Together they danced, a citrus glow.

The teacups juggled in a line,
While spoons complained, 'We should dine!'
But laughter won, they spun around,
Creating joy without a sound.

Acceptance blooms in oddest forms,
Like socks and spoons in playful storms.
So let us cheer for quirks, you see,
In the fabric of life, we're all so free.

The Fabric of Influence

In a world of threads and seams,
We stitch our dreams with crazy beams.
A patchwork tale of every hue,
With every knot, we start anew.

Silly patterns, tangled in glee,
Woven tales of you and me.
Some hold tight, some fly away,
A colorful mess where we play.

Hooks of Heritage

Old family tales hang on the wall,
Each story a hook, each legend a call.
Grandma's yarns, slightly askew,
Warped by time, but still feel true.

In the closet, the past takes flight,
With quirks and quirks, it's quite a sight.
Hats from grandpa, shoes from an aunt,
Strange as they seem, they still enchant.

Snapshots of the Heart

Captured moments, a gallery bright,
Smiles and giggles, a pure delight.
Polaroids dance on the fridge's door,
Each snapshot whispers, 'There's so much more!'

In laughter's frame, the joy is clear,
Every click tells tales we hold dear.
Life's a collage of silly faces,
Making memories in quirky places.

The Weave of Purpose

Threads of intent all intertwined,
With a twist and a turn, we often find.
A tapestry rich, with colors bold,
Each choice a stitch in the tale we told.

With every pull, a lesson learned,
In layers of fabric, our passions burned.
So here's to the fun of creating this right,
Weaving our stories, day and night.

The Little Things That Bind

In the pocket of my mind,
A stray thread I did find.
It pulled at my attention,
A curious invention.

A mismatched sock on my floor,
Holds secrets I can't ignore.
With each color, a tale spun,
Of laughs and days of fun.

The clasp of a quirky charm,
A story that can disarm.
It jangled with a grin,
Each time my shoe slipped in.

In the drawer where chaos reigns,
Dance the joys and little pains.
With a giggle and a cheer,
Life's silly threads are near.

Sewn Sentiments

A needle with a wink and twist,
Stitches love when we can't resist.
In threads that tangle with a spark,
Lies the joy beneath the lark.

I pulled a stitch, it snapped with glee,
It said, 'Hey, how about some tea?'
With whims and fancies that collide,
Crafting memories side by side.

A patch from when life was a riot,
The joys of chaos can't deny it.
Each seam a giggle, each fold a laugh,
In the fabric of our silly path.

So here's to the quirks and the seams,
Where laughter weaves the best of dreams.
In every stitch, we find delight,
Sewn sentiments, our hearts ignite.

The Weight of Connection

A button popped, but not in vain,
It whispers secrets loud as rain.
It anchors tales from days gone by,
Holding memories that amplify.

With a twist and a playful pull,
Life's connections can be full.
Sometimes loose, and sometimes tight,
Each bond a giggle in the night.

A colorful clasp upon my coat,
Sings of clumsy little notes.
It flaps in joy, it dances free,
Laughing at what we can't foresee.

In the tangle of threads we find,
That connection isn't always kind.
Yet with a chuckle and a cheer,
We embrace the weight, year after year.

Unraveled Motives

I found a spool of tangled thought,
With every twist, I'm overwrought.
Unraveled tales in vivid hue,
Plotting mischief just for you.

A playful jab at knotted strings,
Each woven note, a song that sings.
With little quirks and silly rhymes,
We dance on mismatched, joyful times.

The motivation behind the mess,
A laugh that turns into success.
In the fabric of our playful play,
Lies the smiles we weave each day.

So here's to threads that come undone,
In the laughter shared, we find our fun.
With silly knots and playful seams,
Life uncovers its wildest dreams.

An Ode to Closure

In a world of loops and ties,
Some things stick, while others fly.
You clasp them tight, your hopes in hand,
While others tumble, like grains of sand.

A latch that squeaks, a catch that holds,
In quirky ways, our stories unfold.
With laughter shared and mishaps bright,
We find our way, through day and night.

The Knot of Understanding

Tangled yarns in playful spins,
Twists and turns where laughter begins.
We laugh at ties that seem so grand,
Yet sometimes slip right from our hand.

My friend says, 'Look, I've tied this bow!',
But on the first breeze, it lets go.
We chuckle at the knotted mess,
In these small battles, we're truly blessed.

Threads of Hope

With every stitch, we weave our dreams,
In vibrant colors and playful themes.
But oh, what fun when tangles arise,
A game of patience, a grand surprise!

We pull and tug, then laugh out loud,
For what is life without a crowd?
In every loop, a story told,
Of dreams entwined and hearts of gold.

Secured Sentiments

A button here, a button there,
Some pop right off, others in despair.
We stitch together our daily joys,
While dodging chaos like little boys.

With each attachment, a tale to share,
In hiccups and twirls, we dance on air.
So let us fasten our laughter tight,
In the quirkiest, jolliest of nights.

The New Garment of Conviction

My shirt of choices, so bright and bold,
Stitched with laughter, tales retold.
Every patch a story, every seam a dream,
Worn with pride, or so it would seem.

In pockets of doubt, I stash my fears,
Yet wear them lightly, through the years.
Threadbare ideas, frays in my mind,
A fashion of thoughts, uniquely designed.

Light and Shade in the Weave

In the fabric of life, with colors so bright,
A twist of humor, threading the night.
Sewing on laughter, a patch here and there,
Hiding the wrinkles with great flair.

Sunshine and shadows, a lively dance,
Every roll of the dice, a quirky chance.
I'll wear my awkwardness as if it's chic,
Fashioned with giggles, not a hint of bleak.

Pinched Together by Longing

Sewn are the dreams that tug at my heart,
In seams of humor, they play their part.
Wishing upon a star, a button falls free,
Catching my hopes, like a wild jubilee.

With every stitch, a whimsy unwinds,
Cuddled in fabric, my joy finds.
Laughter stitched tightly, puffing my soul,
Fashioned through longing, I'm feeling whole.

The Weaving of Wishes

Spun from desires, oh let's have a ball,
Kooky creations, we'll make them all.
Laces of laughter, twinkling in glee,
Crafted with wishes, wild and free.

Tangles of hopes, the loom starts to sway,
Each thread a dream that won't fade away.
Interwoven giggles, the fabric of me,
Dancing in colors, joyful and free.

Stitched Together in Belief.

In a world where fasteners hold tight,
Hilarity blooms, twinkling bright.
Some cling to thoughts like double stitch,
While others unravel without a hitch.

With safety pins all in a row,
They patch their doubts, putting on a show.
Giggling at ideas that won't quite fit,
Crafting beliefs, a whimsical bit.

Each thread a tale, a pantomime spin,
We dance on seams, let the laughter begin.
Worn out fabric, yet stories unfold,
In the needle's eye, our secrets are told.

So let's sew together, a patchwork of glee,
Tangle the threads, set our minds free.
With snips and snags, no reason to fret,
In this quirky quilt, no rules to be met.

The Fasteners of Faith

A snap here, a clip there, what a sight!
Fasteners giggle, holding on tight.
With every tug, a comical cheer,
Beliefs hold steady amidst the cheer.

In zippers and buttons, the fun unfolds,
Misfit ideas, like stories retold.
Some squeeze in snug, while others go wide,
It's a hilarious journey, an absurd ride.

Twists and turns, the fabric bends,
Silly concoctions, where laughter blends.
Adhesive quirks, a slapstick plot,
Fasteners wiggle, giving it all they've got.

So let's hold on to what makes us jest,
These playful ideas, they always invest.
For in every clasp, there's a chuckle to find,
A tapestry woven with a whimsical mind.

Threads of Conviction

Bright threads weave through the fabric of dreams,
Silly connections, bursting at the seams.
Tangled opinions in a crafty delight,
Tickling the mind, oh what a sight!

With each wobbly knot, we giggle and cheer,
Strange convictions nestled oh-so-near.
Some claim to know, while others just grin,
In this merry dance, let the fun begin!

Yarns unravel as laughter ensues,
Crafting beliefs, a colorful ruse.
The fabric of life, awash with surprise,
In every thread, a jest in disguise.

So let's stitch our quirks, in patterns unique,
In this playful tapestry, it's joy we seek.
With every twist and turn, we'll never be lost,
For in the threads, lies the fun at no cost!

Whispers Beneath the Surface

Beneath the layers, a chuckle brews,
Hidden ideas, in joyous hues.
Muffled laughter, like fabric in folds,
Secrets of thought that the surface upholds.

A tickle of whimsy, lightly it grips,
Like a playful thread that forever tips.
Underlying truths in a jester's guise,
Each whisper a joke, under starlit skies.

With antics and antics, the words play hide,
In seams of belief, they take us for rides.
Words that stumble, fall flat and rise,
Mirth echoing softly, a bond in disguise.

So lean in close, hear the laughter surround,
In the whispers of fabric, joy multiplies, profound.
For beneath every layer, a jest to uncover,
Like the tales of old, still charmingly clever.

The Architecture of Acceptance

In a world where quirks collide,
Some wear hats, others hide.
Big pockets hold their secrets tight,
While laughter blooms in daylight.

Crooked ties and mismatched shoes,
In this style, no one can lose.
Patterns clash, but we're all kin,
A tapestry where smiles begin.

Oddities dance, twirl, and spin,
Each with a story, a cheeky grin.
With color galore, no dull affair,
Fashion faux pas, we do not care.

So gather round and take a chance,
Join the fun, let's break the stance.
For in this chaos, joy will rise,
Creating joy in every guise.

The Interlocking of Ideas

Thoughts entwined, a silly mess,
Each one claims it's the best guess.
They bump and jostle, laugh and shout,
In this bouncy house of doubt.

Perspectives clash like candy canes,
Debates sprout like wild, funny veins.
Silly notions soar like kites,
Tickling brains in neon lights.

One says blue, the other red,
Cerebral circus in each head.
Yet through the babble, giggles frolic,
In this tangle, oh so comic.

So grab a thought, take a dive,
Join the fun, let ideas thrive.
In this booth of wacky themes,
We stitch together our wild dreams.

Sewn in Silence

Stitches whisper in the night,
Threads are dancing, what a sight!
Each knot a secret, strong and tight,
Sewing dreams with all its might.

Patterns form with sly delight,
Tales are woven, soft and light.
In shadows, laughter threads align,
Creating stitches quite divine.

Corners hide a jest or two,
A wink, a nod, all crafted true.
In this workshop, souls unwind,
As quiet giggles fill the mind.

So let us sew with friendly cheer,
In every stitch, draw someone near.
For in this silence, joy expands,
Like gentle threads from loving hands.

The Tactile Truth

Feel the fabric, rough and bright,
Textures tickle, pure delight.
Cotton whispers to my skin,
A playful dance, let's begin.

Silk slips by, a mischievous tease,
While woolly hugs bring warmth and ease.
In every swatch, a tale is spun,
Crafting laughter, just for fun.

Patterns clash in joyous knots,
Each layer tells the ones that forgot.
In tactile truth, let's be absurd,
Spinning yarns with silly word.

So grab a patch, stitch it right,
In this quilt, it's sheer delight.
For in these textures, funny lives,
Crafted tales where laughter thrives.

The Fabric of Faith

In a world of threads we play,
Each stitch is a silly ballet.
Tangled yarns of thought we weave,
With laughter's grace, we believe.

A patchwork of dreams we wear,
Some fit and some are quite rare.
With every tug, we just can't frown,
It's joy that keeps us worn down.

Closets filled with patterns old,
Stories of warmth and laughs retold.
With whimsy in every seam,
We spin our tales, we dance, we dream.

So let's patch holes of doubt today,
With colors bright in a cheeky way.
It's not about what's good or bad,
But the giggles that we've always had.

Clips and Creeds

With clips that hold my heart so tight,
I dance and twirl, full of delight.
Each charm a tale, a funny spin,
With winks and nods, let quirks begin.

Some fittings snug, some loose and free,
In life's great circus, none agree.
A tongue-in-cheek parade we march,
With comical grace, beneath the arch.

Oh, wear your laughs like a badge,
Even when life's a little mad.
In missing links, we find our style,
That spark of joy, that cheeky smile.

So grab a clip and join the game,
In this wild world, nothing's the same.
Let's keep it light, as life unfolds,
With laughter's gold, our story's told.

Stitches in the Soul

With every stitch, a story spins,
In quirky loops, where laughter grins.
Some seams are tight, and some are loose,
But all together, they're quite the moose.

A needle pokes at thoughts of old,
Tales of whimsy, oh so bold.
We patch our fears with laughter's thread,
And dance around what's left unsaid.

Each fabric piece has tales to share,
In this patchwork quilt of joyful flair.
With every fold, a memory swells,
In giggles wrapped like magical spells.

Let laughter be the yarn we spin,
For every loss, let joy begin.
In this tapestry of silly life,
We find the joy, despite the strife.

The Snap of Tradition

With every snap, the jokes collide,
In history's dance, we laugh with pride.
What once was stiff, now brings a grin,
As we poke fun at where we've been.

Old customs slip like a comical race,
Traditions now wear a cheeky face.
In hilarity, we realign,
Finding joy in the serious line.

That snap of old brings forth a laugh,
With history's quirks, we'll find our path.
As memories jingle with a twist,
In playful moments, we can't resist.

So let us cherish these silly threads,
Where laughter blooms, and joy spreads.
For in each snap, a tale awaits,
With humor bright, our heart elates.

Interlaced Journeys

When threads entwine, oh what a sight,
They twist and turn, a comical flight.
A button's wink, a cheeky grin,
Traveling paths where laughs begin.

Stitching tales of joy and jest,
Adventures woven, never a rest.
Each loop a story, each knot a tease,
In the chaos, we find our ease.

The colors clash and patterns play,
A mismatched dance in a quirky way.
When they collide, there's much to see,
A fabric of laughter, wild and free.

So heed the tales of threads well sewn,
In every twist, a giggle is grown.
With every push, in laughter we glide,
In this crazy quilt, we all reside.

The Ties that Transcend

Oh, how they cling, those crafty ties,
A playful poke, a light surprise.
In every pull, a sudden shift,
Life's little knots can be a gift.

They bind the odd to the unknown,
A curious mix that's often shown.
A loose end flapping, quite the stunt,
In every chaos, we find the fun.

When tangled thoughts take center stage,
Our laughter grows, a carefree rage.
For through the knots, we often see,
The ties that shine so joyfully.

So pull and tug, embrace the mess,
In every twist, we find success.
With every knot that loosens tight,
A chuckle rises, pure delight.

Securing the Simple Truth

As we fasten truths with threads of cheer,
We giggle softly, draw each other near.
With every clasp, a secret shared,
In playful jests, we realize we dared.

Our fabric's strong, but oh so light,
Through laughter's lens, we see the bright.
Each little hook, a gentle jest,
In life's grand tale, we're truly blessed.

When misaligned and slightly askew,
We find the joy in the odd que.
A button's bounce, a twist of fate,
In silly moments, we celebrate.

So stitch a smile, hold tight the fun,
In each silly act, we're never done.
Secure the truth with laughter's thread,
In this merry dance, we're joyfully led.

Unthreaded Understanding

When threads unravel, laughter flows,
In tangled mess, the humor grows.
With every snip, a giggle rings,
In chaos sharp, the joy it brings.

A playful poke at life's designs,
We weave our tales through quirky lines.
Unbuttoned thoughts, they roam about,
In wild pursuits, we laugh and shout.

Those loose ends flailing in the breeze,
Can bring us joy, if we just please.
With every quirk, our hearts align,
Through tangled tales, we twist and shine.

So let's unthread and see what's real,
In silly antics, we find the feel.
With laughter loud, our wisdom grows,
In every mishap, the fun bestows.

The Ties We Wear

In a world of colorful ties,
We wrestle with choices, oh my!
Do we knot them tightly or slack?
Each twist and turn brings a laugh back.

A bow that's crooked, oh what a sight,
Fashion advice? Not tonight!
Stripes and polka dots have a chat,
They argue, but what's wrong with that?

Stitching stories, one thread at a time,
A fashion faux pas is simply sublime.
With every tug and playful pull,
Life's little quirks make it all so full.

So wear your ties however you please,
In this tapestry of giggles and tease.
With laughter sewn into each seam,
Life is richer than we dare to dream.

Fasteners of the Heart

Clasping emotions in a shiny hue,
A snap of affection, just for you.
Each button, each loop, a tale to unfold,
In the fabric of life, let the stories be told.

A zipper that's stuck makes us all pause,
"Help me!" it cries, "This can't be because!
I'm just a mere latch on a jacket so fine,
But deep inside, our laughter shall shine!"

Velcro whispers secrets with every embrace,
As we stick together in this wild race.
The peeling sound is music so sweet,
Sharing our quirks makes us complete.

So let's fasten our joys with flair and with style,
In silly chaos we'll dance for a while.
With a wink and a nod, let's cherish the fun,
For a heart that's unfastened is never done.

Secured in Shadows

In the corners where laughter hides,
A safety pin holds all our sides.
With frayed edges and colors so bright,
We stumble through laughter into the light.

Tangled in threads, our stories all weave,
A patchwork of moments we choose to believe.
In the quiet of night when things go awry,
A button pops off and we all start to sigh.

Lurking in shadows, we chuckle and roar,
As we search for the bits that we've lost on the floor.
Giggling at mischief, we stitch up the past,
Binding our tales in stitches that last.

So let's toast to the fastening of fate,
And laugh at the trouble; it's never too late.
In a world that's a puzzle, so grand and so bold,
Each piece that we find is a treasure to hold.

Where Fabric Meets Faith

In a world stitched together with grace,
We find what we believe in this cozy space.
A hem full of hopes, some frayed at the seam,
Yet magic unfolds in this whimsical dream.

Quilted affirmations, patchwork of thoughts,
Each color has meaning and laughter it bought.
As seams twist and turn, we gather and spin,
With fabric in hand, let the fun times begin!

A fabric of stories, all tangled and spun,
We dance in the threads, embracing the fun.
With laughter we gather, each missing piece found,
Stitching together our joy all around.

So let our hearts roam in patterns so vast,
Where the stitches of faith hold the moments that last.
In this playful tapestry, we'll find our way,
With threads of delight that brighten the day.

Stitched Notions

In a tailor's shop, all quite absurd,
Threads talk gossip, oh how they've heard.
A patch says, 'I'm perfect, just look at my seam!'
While the snags chuckle, 'Life's never a dream.'

Stitching together all sorts of quirks,
And yet, they all dance like dapper little jerks.
The thimble chimes in, quite full of cheer,
'Life's just a fabric, let's stitch it here!'

The Clasp of Certainty

A hook and a latch, so tightly they scheme,
'With us,' they declare, 'you'll live out your dream!'
But the buttons laugh, 'Oh, look at them fight!
We pop off each day, a true comedic sight.'

The belt winks with a twist and a slide,
'You strap on your faith, but do you abide?'
You can feel secure, or a total misfit,
It seems the real answer is just in the split!

Little Mementos of Morality

A pin stands rigid, with an air of advice,
'Tackling issues, oh isn't it nice?'
But the loose threads giggle, they've seen much worse,
'Try holding a secret, it's a delicate curse!'

The safety clip whispers, 'I'll keep you so safe,
But don't get too close or I'll end up a waif.'
In the drawers of life, where the odd things lay,
A thimble just sighs, 'Can we rethink our play?'

Doubt's Fastening

A buckle that wiggles, unsure of its goal,
'Am I holding tight, or losing control?'
The zippers are nervous, they jingle in doubt,
'Let's zip it up quick, before we fall out!'

The snaps won't commit, they just go 'pop'!
'What if we fumble, will we really stop?'
Clips clutter and clank, with a raucous cheer,
'Embrace all the chaos, let's fasten with fear!'

Small Wonders of Assurance

Tiny fasteners hold us tight,
In pockets, they make things right.
A pop, a snap, a joyful cheer,
Stitching together what we hold dear.

In coats and bags, they play their role,
Keeping our secrets, oh so whole.
A wink and a nudge, a little tease,
Life's quirky quirks put us at ease.

Giggles come when they lose their way,
Rolling beneath the couch to play.
Each little piece, a tiny jest,
Creating a laugh, we feel so blessed.

So here's to the knickknacks we adore,
They bind our dreams, and so much more.
With smiles and winks, let's celebrate,
The tiny things that make us great!

The Fabric of Belief

In threads of joy, we sew our fate,
A flick of fabric, can't be late.
Twirls and whirls, a dance in thread,
Each stitch a laugh, our hearts are led.

Pockets full of oddities bright,
Holding the quirks that feel so right.
A dash of color, a hint of flair,
Fiddling with threads, without a care.

When yarns unravel, what a sight!
We chuckle as we battle the fright.
With needle in hand, we smile and jest,
It's all a game, we're truly blessed.

So grab a spool and join the fun,
Let's weave our tales, till day is done.
In each little loop, a giggle resides,
The fabric of life, where laughter abides!

Interwoven Certainties

In tangled threads, our fates entwine,
We craft our stories, oh so fine.
A snip, a tie, a playful dare,
Each twist and turn brings joy to share.

With every loop, we grasp our dreams,
In vibrant hues, the laughter beams.
Fiddling with quirks that come our way,
Life's little jests brighten the day.

A tangle here, a knot to splice,
We giggle and grin, isn't it nice?
In the fabric of chaos, we find our glee,
Slipping and sliding, carefree as can be.

So here's to the mishaps, a humorous dance,
In all that we wear, let's take a chance.
For in every stitch, we find what's true,
Laughter and love, all stitched through and through!

Sewn into the Soul

In every fabric, a story spun,
Life's little antics, laugh and run.
Tightly stitched with care and glee,
Crafted moments, wild and free.

A misaligned patch, what a show,
We giggle and chuckle as we go.
Each quirky stitch, a memory made,
In the tapestry of life, we wade.

The colors clash, but what a sight!
Each error turns laughter, pure delight.
With threads of joy, we mend and weave,
Through laughter, we learn, and we believe.

So let's bind our lives with smiles and cheer,
In this fabric of madness, we hold dear.
With needle and thread, we find our role,
Creating a quilt, sewn into the soul!

The Undercurrent of Resolve

In a world where oddities dwell,
A sock without a pair, oh well!
They mingle in the laundry dance,
A fabric fate, a wink, a prance.

As mismatched as a penguin's flipper,
They still embrace each little sticker.
One's a heart, the other a star,
Together they frolic, near and far.

A paperclip's dream of lofty heights,
Beside a thumbtack's daring flights.
In pockets deep or drawers confined,
They rally, laughter well-defined.

A button eyed its wearer bold,
Said, "Stay fast, let stories unfold!"
And with that, came a giggling spree,
As they sang of bonds, wild and free.

Connections Unseen

Yo-yo strings and marble spins,
In the chaos, chuckles begin.
A pen that never needs to write,
Jumps to life – oh what a sight!

The jingle from a keychain's spree,
Mumbles secrets, oh so free.
A wallet thick with dreams untold,
Crafts a tale that never gets old.

A spoon with trust in every scoop,
Joins a fork in daring loop.
Together they twirl in pots so deep,
Cooking up giggles, secrets to keep.

Threads of laughter softly weave,
In garments stitched, we all believe.
Even mismatched, they share a cheer,
For love and joy are always near.

Lifting the Veil of Doubt

A rubber band with gusto seeks,
To launch itself, as laughter peaks.
Who knew it would stretch beyond the line,
And show us all that joy's divine?

A paper crane made from an old receipt,
Dreams of flight, oh so sweet!
It flutters by a tape roll's side,
Both giggling as they glide and bide.

Stickers stuck to the fridge's face,
Sway with pride in their stickered place.
Each peeling edge brings tales anew,
For every mark can tell what's true.

And still, that quirky fridge hums loud,
Crafting a tune, a jovial crowd.
In the simplest things, we find our clout,
As silly scenes lift every doubt.

Strung Along in Faith

A necklace made from spaghetti strands,
Finds meaning in the silliest hands.
Worn proudly at a grand buffet,
"Can you taste this?" it laughs away.

A shoelace tied in triple loops,
Holds together all the goofball troops.
They trip, they laugh, they tumble down,
The ground's the stage, no room for frown.

A tin can's call, old strings attached,
Whispers secrets tightly matched.
With echoes of misplaced designs,
They share the giggles in their lines.

As laughter stitches through each seam,
There's magic, joy, and hope's bright beam.
When bound together, come what may,
Each little piece finds its own way.

Hidden Attachments

In the drawer of my mind's delight,
Lie items that give a curious fright.
Lost socks and trinkets, all out of place,
Tangled tales leave a grin on my face.

Under the bed, a chaos so grand,
Each relic a story, just underhand.
One's a knight with a history so bold,
Playing hide and seek with treasures of old.

The cat stalks around, a judge of our fun,
As I trip on a shoe—oh, isn't life a pun?
With each step I take, I stumble and fall,
Wonders of nonsense, amusing us all.

So gather your goodies, let laughter ensue,
For messiness sparkles, a joke in plain view.
In this whimsical world with secrets to share,
The joy of attachments is everywhere there.

A Tangle of Truths

A spaghetti of stories, all knotted and tight,
Playful confessions that dance in the light.
Whispers of logic wrapped up in a sprawl,
A merry confusion where laughter stands tall.

With yarn and with laughter, we weave in delight,
Each tale spins a circle, a topsy-turvy flight.
A sock claims to know why the fridge is so cold,
While a whistle insists it's a secret untold.

The cat meows loudly, demanding a say,
In the nonsense parade that unfolds every day.
Is it real, is it fake? Who can even determine?
In our tangled beliefs, the truth starts to squirm in.

So let's toast to the chaos that binds us as one,
To truths wrapped in laughter, it's all in good fun.
For tangled thoughts matter with friends by your side,
In the web of our minds, we find truth can hide.

Fastened Feelings

Tightly sewn patches for hearts on the mend,
A quirk in the stitching where laughter can blend.
Each loop tells a story, a slip or a slip,
While memories jingle with joy on a trip.

The buttons we choose hold more than they show,
A wink and a nod, oh, the secrets they know!
From the odd to the funny, they each have a zest,
Bringing out giggles, they're truly the best.

The haphazard outfits we dare to display,
Bring smiles in the neighborhood, brightening the day.
With colors so wild and patterns that clash,
Our fashion faux pas become quite the bash!

So let's wear our oddments with hearty pride,
In a world of fast feelings, let's take a wild ride.
For joy is the thread that holds us all near,
Fastened in laughter, we've nothing to fear!

Woven Whispers

In the loom of the night where dreams take a spin,
Threads of our stories begin to intertwine.
A whisper that giggles as it flutters by,
Unfolding the secrets with a mischievous eye.

The tapestry of lives, a colorful net,
Holds memories precious that we won't forget.
From the mischief of childhood to late-night chats,
Each stitch is a tale where the humor just bats.

So gather around in this fabric of fun,
With laughter as glue, it's a race never run.
In the yarns that we spin, we find we belong,
A chorus of chuckles, our whimsical song.

For woven together, we dance and we weave,
In a world stitched with joy, we learn to believe.
Every laugh is a thread, making us stronger,
In this splendid tapestry, we'll laugh even longer.

The Close of Common Threads

In a world so stitched with dreams,
Some seams are tighter than they seem.
A button here, a string undone,
Laughing at the fray, we run.

When conversations start to fray,
A pop of laughter leads the way.
With every tug, the fabric sways,
Let's keep it light, through all the plays.

Sometimes we twist, sometimes we bend,
Yet moments shared are easiest to mend.
With threads around, we're never apart,
A patchwork quilt, a stitched-up heart.

So here's to laughter in the loop,
To tangled thoughts, a jolly troupe.
In every stitch, a tale we share,
In the tapestry of life, we care.

Woven Threads of Understanding

In a fabric thick with tales untold,
We weave humor, bright and bold.
Like yarn that tangles, laughs will bloom,
In every fiber, there's simply room.

A needle slips, we laugh aloud,
At every wobble, we feel so proud.
Hues of friendship, all entwined,
In this crazy quilt, we're aligned.

So stitch by stitch, with joy we create,
A silly tapestry, it's never too late.
With threads of laughter warming our days,
We navigate life in whimsical ways.

Look close and see the magic woven,
In tangled threads, our hearts have chosen.
Each knot and loop, a reason to giggle,
In the grand fabric, let's dance and wriggle.

The Resolve to Hold On

In the tight-knit group of quirk divine,
We promise patience over wine.
With fraying edges, we clutch so tight,
Bantering jokes into the night.

When threads unspool from reckless hands,
We tie them back with zany plans.
With laughter loud, we steer our course,
In knots of joy, we feel the force.

Against the pull of topics bleak,
We rally round with chuckles unique.
In every twist, we find a way,
To hold on tight and laugh all day.

Undone by time, but never fear,
We patch our hearts with love and cheer.
In silly stitches, we will trust,
Through every rip, it's love we must.

Tackled Thoughts

With freestyles spun from fabric fun,
We tackle dreams, we're on the run.
In every thought, a comedy waits,
Twists and turns of open gates.

So here we go, with a punchline's grace,
As fabric sways in this funny race.
From mismatched patches, laughter brews,
In awkward stitches, we find our muse.

When thoughts get tangled, we simply grin,
For messy threads let humor in.
With every stitch, the craziness grows,
In our patchwork minds, anything goes.

Let's dive headfirst into the fray,
With jests and japes to light the way.
In tackled thoughts, we find our flight,
In every twist, we feel so right.

Latching on to Hope

In a world where loops entwine,
A little clasp knows just the sign.
It holds the fabric, tight and round,
A jester's giggle—joy is found.

With winks and flaps, it wobbles proud,
A hat that's worn amidst the crowd.
The silly patterns! Bright and bold,
Each twist a tale, each fold a gold.

The Click of Assurance

A snap, a click, a joyful sound,
As confidence leaps off the ground.
Like puzzles played, it fits just right,
Each pop a cheer, pure delight!

When doubts come creeping, don't you fret,
Just hear the click, let worries set.
It muffles fears with a playful tune,
A rhythm that dances under the moon.

Stitched Together by Dreams

Threads of laughter weave the night,
In patterns strange, but oh so bright!
Each stitch a chuckle, every seam,
A wacky quilt—a twinkling dream.

With a tap and tug, it starts to hum,
A symphony of 'whoops' and 'yum!'
It sparkles with colors, lively and keen,
An artful chaos fit for a queen!

Tangible Tokens of Trust

A shiny charm from days gone by,
Worn on a collar, oh so spry.
With every glance, it kicks to life,
This silly charm amused with strife.

In playful whispers, truths are found,
As giggles and snorts bounce around.
These little keepsakes remind us we're here,
In laughter's embrace—nothing to fear!

The Loop of Loyalty

In a world where colors clash,
A circle swirls, a friendly bash.
Threads are tangled, laughter wide,
A dance of trust, we slip and glide.

With every twist, a joy unfolds,
Tales of friendship, jests retold.
Yet, in the fray, a shoe gets tossed,
Amidst the giggles, nothing's lost.

Secure in the Unknown

In pockets deep, odd treasures hide,
Old tickets, gum, a twist of pride.
What lies beneath? A mystery bright,
As we reach in, our giggles ignite.

A sock here, a coin there, what a find!
Each whimsy's charm is nicely aligned.
In the chaos, joy takes flight,
For in the strange, we feel just right.

Patterns of Perception

Polka dots and stripes collide,
In wacky ways, they coincide.
A spotted frog on a plaid chair,
Who knew odd pairs could make us stare?

Through mismatched frames, we view the scene,
Laughing at things that once seemed mean.
In quirky sights and silly dreams,
Life's a puzzle, bursting at the seams.

The Gathered Heartstrings

Tangled yarn holds secrets tight,
Each knot a giggle in the night.
With goofy tales we gather 'round,
In every loop, our joy is found.

A wink, a grin, a playful tug,
We cheer for hearts, so snug as a bug.
Though threads may fray, their strength is clear,
In this lightness, we hold dear.

The Interlude of Belonging

In a drawer they dance, all so bright,
Jumbling together, a quirky sight.
They have stories to share, if we lend an ear,
Each tiny tab holds a hint of cheer.

In pockets they linger, in coats they play,
Sometimes they vanish, just to sway.
With laughter like squeaks, they burst into view,
Chasing the lost, like a merry crew.

They join at the seams, causing tugs and pulls,
Mismatched and goofy, like a pack of fools.
A rainbow of memories sewn on our thread,
They're just here for fun, no need for dread.

So here's to the jests, all tangled and free,
A playful reminder of camaraderie.
Let's laugh at the chaos; it's how we unite,
In the world of small things, everything's bright.

Calibrated Dreams

A floaty notion, like a pie in the sky,
With misfit shapes that all try to fly.
They swirl in a dance, oh so merry,
Each one a puzzle, unique and cheery.

From pockets to cushions, they scatter about,
A peek into dreams, what life's all about.
They giggle and twinkle, a sight to behold,
As they tumble together, bright stories unfold.

A flicker of laughter ignites the night,
Each playful glimpse makes mundane feel right.
No chart to follow, just whimsy in sight,
Every odd piece makes joy take flight.

So let's join the jest, embrace the slight mess,
In the realm of nonsense, we find happiness.
A journey of giggles, let's skip down the lane,
With our whimsical finds, we'll never complain.

The Clasp of Certainty

A wink at the corner, a nod in return,
They hold it together, with passion they burn.
Though mismatched at times, they still know their role,
A quirky adventure, they make us whole.

In clinks and in clatters, a riotous sound,
They cling without effort, tightly wound.
Through wiggles and jiggles, they effortlessly bind,
An orchestra of jests, in mischief they find.

They clamor for order, yet love the absurd,
Creating a humor that's rarely deferred.
A clasp here and there, a humorous twist,
In the gallery of life, it seldom gets missed.

So let's play along, with a giggle or two,
In this clasp of madness, there's joy that's true.
Embrace the confusion, give chaos a cheer,
With every little clasp, laughter draws near.

Emblems of the Heart

In pockets they dwell, a mismatched brigade,
With tales of their journeys, they never fade.
The quirks of the past, in colors and threads,
Reduce life's heavy woes to light-hearted spreads.

They jingle and jangle, the sound of delight,
Each one a token, a symbol of light.
Though some may be missing, and others unsure,
The mix feels just right; it's laughter we ensure.

An emblem of winks, a cheeky old jest,
Together in chaos, they do what they best.
From heartfelt connections to giggles that beam,
They stitch up our world with whimsical dream.

So here's to the team, the wild and the bright,
That captures the magic in the dead of night.
With these charms of the heart, let's dance and depart,
For in every small thing lies a brand new start.

Clasping Tiny Truths

Little things we hold so tight,
They make us giggle, day and night.
A quirky clasp, a painted hue,
We find our joy in what we do.

A tiny hook, a playful catch,
Like silly jokes that start to hatch.
We swear it's true, but who's to blame?
For each odd truth, it's just the same!

Sometimes they pop, they fly away,
Yet still we laugh, come what may.
A treasure trove of absurd schemes,
We stitch our lives with patchy dreams.

So grab your truth and hold it fast,
With wiggles, giggles, good times amassed.
Through tiny grips, we take our flight,
In every laugh, finds our delight!

The Stitch of Certainty

An errant thread in life's big seam,
Wobbles and bends, oh what a dream!
I thought it straight, yet here it loops,
Like daring squirrels in silly groups.

I sew my doubts with colors bright,
A patchwork joke, a whimsical sight.
Each knot a giggle, each tie a jest,
Crafting chaos, I do my best.

A needle's dance with laughter shared,
In every stitch, surprise ensnared.
Who knew the truth could tangle so,
While in this fabric, we steal the show?

So join the fun in this grand chase,
In every seam, we find our place.
With every poke and playful tug,
We stitch our memories, oh so snug!

Fastened Thoughts

A whimsical mind with thoughts like glue,
Sticking together, a colorful crew.
With pins and clips, our ideas cling,
We jump and jive, oh what a fling!

Unruly dreams that wobble and sway,
Each one a jest that wants to play.
Like paperclips that dance around,
In this wild circus, joy is found.

They slide and slip, but never fall,
Our thoughts alive, we love them all.
In every twist, there's laughter loud,
Fastened tightly, we feel so proud.

So grab your thoughts and hold them tight,
With playful nudges, take your flight.
In this parade of silly cheer,
We fasten joy, it's crystal clear!

Fragile Connections

A delicate thread binds us with glee,
We twirl and twist, like leaves from a tree.
In this ballet of awkward grace,
Every stumble finds a smiling face.

We link our quirks with laughter bright,
Dancing around through day and night.
A gentle tug, a silly sigh,
In our sweet chaos, we learn to fly.

Each wobble sparkles, each jolt's a jest,
In fragile bonds, we feel our best.
Though storms may rattle and winds may shout,
These funny ties we never doubt.

So cherish the threads that bind us tight,
In this joyful mess, we take our flight.
With every giggle, our hearts expand,
In fragile joy, we take a stand!

Intertwined Aspirations

In a world of mismatched socks,
Dreams hang like laundry on the blocks.
Hopes stitched with a child's delight,
Youthful giggles, oh what a sight.

They twirl around like dancing threads,
Tales imagined in cozy beds.
Mismatched goals, oh how they tangle,
Yet laughter's light, we always wrangle.

Every aim, a quirky design,
Crafted over coffee and cake divine.
With yarns of joy we boldly mix,
Silly schemes, a playful fix.

The fabric of wishes gets so bright,
In our whims, there's pure delight.
So let it be, a funny lore,
Interlaced dreams, forevermore.

The Heft of the Unseen

Carrying hopes beneath our hats,
Shuffling through with chattering chats.
Invisible loads, a jolly spree,
What's hidden deep, no one can see.

Emotions weigh more than a ton,
Yet we giggle, just having fun.
Wear your grin like a sturdy belt,
The heft of joy is truly felt.

Behind those eyes, a riot of plans,
A silent dance of silly stans.
With every chuckle, the weight does lift,
Unseen treasures, our greatest gift.

So come, let's quirkily combine,
Our silly thoughts, perfectly align.
Laughing at what we cannot show,
Together we thrive, as we ebb and flow.

Threads of Time

A clock made of candy and dreams,
Where seconds tick with giggly themes.
Each moment, a thread in a quilt so bright,
Stitched with mischief, a pure delight.

The past may fray like worn-out seams,
But we weave stories, bright as beams.
Tickles of laughter, echoes so grand,
In this tapestry, hand in hand.

The future unfolds like a silly prank,
Each wish we cast, a little tank.
Revved up engines of hope in flight,
Crashing in giggles, oh what a sight!

So let's gather all our tangled yarn,
And spin silly tales from dusk till dawn.
With every knot, a chuckle's born,
Threads of time, in joy we're sworn.

The Charm of Small Things

A pebble tossed can cause a splash,
Or make a whisper with a dash.
Tiny wonders we lightly find,
In a world so grand, sweetly entwined.

The tick of bugs is a merry beat,
Little joys dance on wobbly feet.
A feather drops; we laugh and play,
Charming moments in a big ol' way.

Each crumb we share becomes a feast,
From simple bites, our smiles released.
So let the laughter jump and swing,
In the treasure of small, let's all take wing.

For every giggle, a magic brings,
Unseen forces that laughter flings.
In life's embrace, we start to sing,
So cherish the charm in small, tiny things.

Glistening Pledges

In the drawer, colors collide,
Promises shimmer, a sudden ride.
Whimsical shapes, odd and round,
Lively laughter, joy is found.

A tiny sphere, a grand request,
To hold together what's at its best.
The quirky crew, they chat and tease,
Grabbing fortunes from mortared knees.

They sparkle bright, like eyes at night,
Binding secrets, a humorous sight.
Each twist and turn, a little prank,
Where giggles bounce, and hopes rank.

With every click, a tale unfolds,
A friendship stitched with laughter bold.
In this playful world, we conspire,
To fasten dreams that won't expire.

The Buttons We Choose

A button here, a button there,
Decisions made with playful flair.
Tiny diplomats in a row,
Mismatched comrades putting on a show.

Each selection brings a grin,
A zany battle, where to begin?
Shiny, matte, or feel so grand,
The laughter grows, it's all unplanned.

Connecting fabric of our days,
With tales of joy and silly ways.
One winks, another starts to jig,
In this odd dance, we're all so big.

So twist and tug, don't take too long,
Join the chorus of our merry song.
In every clasp, there's light and cheer,
A button's charm, forever dear.

Beneath the Fabric of Belonging

Stitches tight, yet spirits roam,
Underneath, we find our home.
Each little circle, a quirky clan,
In this wild game, we're all the fan.

We gather round, a motley crew,
Dressed in colors, silly and true.
Pulling threads from yesterday's tale,
Unraveling mirth, we shall not fail.

Giggles hide in seams so small,
Under the layers, we stand tall.
We swap and share with joyful glee,
A thread of fun, connecting thee.

In the warmth of laughter and light,
Our fabric dances, day and night.
With every twist, our hearts align,
In these smiles, our bonds define.

Fastening Thoughts to Reality

With a click, we snap the day,
Thoughts held tight in a funny way.
Each little piece a wild delight,
In this game of wrong and right.

We take our dreams, make them bold,
Stitching stories, mighty and old.
Fanciful notions take their stance,
In this merry world, we dance.

A flicker here, a jabber there,
Fastening whims into the air.
Each quirky move, a step we make,
With laughter stitched, there's no mistake.

So gather round, let's tie it down,
In every chuckle, wear the crown.
Reality bends, though we may joke,
With hooks and clips, our hearts evoke.

The Fabricated Facade

With a stitch here and a seam there,
We dress our thoughts with utmost care.
Like a clown with shoes two sizes wide,
We trip on truths we try to hide.

In levity's lap, we weave and twine,
Throwing fabric decisions like cheap wine.
A patch for every awkward truth,
We wear our quirks like jester's sleuth.

The colors clash and patterns fight,
Yet somehow it all feels just right.
Our crazy quilt of laugh and sigh,
Won't mend if we never try.

So let's embrace the seams we bear,
And dance like nobody has a care.
With snickers sewn in every fold,
The stories of our lives unfold.

The Pulse of Connection

In every hold, a pulse we find,
A clasp of joy, a twist of mind.
With mismatched threads, we draw the line,
A tie that binds and feels divine.

Tangled up in laughter's cheer,
We boost our spirits, spreading near.
With every jab and playful tease,
We know our hearts can only please.

The fabric of our daily grind,
Woven close, yet rarely aligned.
Still laughter loops like endless yarn,
We stitch our lives, never to mourn.

Embrace the chaos, it feels so right,
With giggles echoing through the night.
For life's a tapestry, bold and bright,
Crafted by hearts in shared delight.

Threaded Intent

In the grand design of the day,
We thread our feelings in playful sway.
A tug of laughter, a poke of fun,
Crafting how our stories run.

With every stitch, a truth unfolds,
In every hue, a tale retold.
We mix and match, create a mess,
In our cloth, we find success.

The whims we weave, the patterns play,
In this fabric, we're never gray.
We chuckle at quirks, embrace the weird,
Through tangled lives, we are endeared.

So grab your thread, let's make a knot,
With every whimsy, give it a shot.
For together we sew in fabric bright,
Creating joy from the day to night.

A Symphony of Small Things

In a world of tiny bits that cling,
We compose a tune from every fling.
A button here, a snap right there,
Together we find harmony to share.

Each little note in vibrant hue,
Is a chorus full of 'me' and 'you.'
We dance in circles, twirl in place,
The symphony of our joyful embrace.

With laughter stitched into each key,
We play mistakes so wildly free.
For in our rhythm, all is well,
The music tells a tale to tell.

So let's create, let's never cease,
Finding laughs in moments of peace.
For in the small, the grand will sing,
An endless joy of little things.

Fasteners of Faith

In a drawer where oddities lie,
A single clasp caught my eye.
It's shiny, yet holds not much weight,
Like dreams of a first date.

Stitching stories with a twine,
Of moments lost and oh-so-fine.
I wear my quirks like a badge,
Though sometimes they cause a splash.

With every hook and little hook,
I'm searching for that secret nook.
Where laughter bursts like popping seams,
And life unfolds in silly dreams.

A patchwork quilt of jest and cheer,
I find the humor crystal clear.
In every latch that holds me tight,
I twirl and dance into the night.

The Thread of Conviction

Tangled threads upon the floor,
Each one tells a tale of yore.
One's a ribbon, shiny, bright,
The other's frayed, but holds on tight.

With every tug, my heartstrings flutter,
And sometimes I just end up in clutter.
I tie my hopes with a wobbly knot,
Throw in some laughter, give it a shot.

When life's a stitch, and things unwind,
I grab my needle, it's time to bind.
The fabric of fate is nothing but fun,
A patchwork of joy since day one.

So let's embrace the colorful mess,
And find the humor in each distress.
For in every loop and twist we find,
A chance to laugh and not be blind.

Ties that Bind

In the garden where ties do sway,
I chase the whims of a sunny day.
Some are ribbons, others rope,
All are stitched with a hint of hope.

A shoelace here, a belt loop there,
Together, we dance without a care.
I trip and stumble, yet I grin,
For the best part's where we begin.

Each twist and turn makes me chuckle,
Life's like a jigsaw, a daring puzzle.
With every knot, we weave our tale,
And laugh at moments that make us pale.

So let's tie ourselves to joy today,
Before the threads just slip away.
For in jumbled yarn, the fun we find,
Is the secret of hearts that are truly kind.

Closure in Chaos

In a world where everything's askew,
I search for closures, I really do.
Some fit snug, while others slide,
Creating chaos, a wild ride.

A twisty thing, a button, a snap,
Life's like a dress caught in a trap.
I laugh out loud when things get tight,
Wishing for calm, yet craving the fight.

Each bumpy road leads to a laugh,
And I often end up on my other half.
Unraveled yarns in a tangled mess,
But oh, what fun with all this excess!

So here's to closure in all the crazy,
Finding joy in moments a bit hazy.
For even in knots, there lies delight,
With laughter shining through the night.

Tightly Wound Tales

In a drawer, things tangle and spin,
A sock creeps out, a rebellion begins.
Lost in the chaos, a romance ignites,
With a tumble of threads on wild moonlit nights.

The mischief brews as they dance on the floor,
A pin cushion grins, 'I've seen this before!'
Needles get tangled, a heist on the run,
And laughter erupts - oh, this is such fun!

Stitches can tear when we take a wrong turn,
But a patchwork of giggles is all that we yearn.
With fabric and flair, our stories we weave,
In a world full of whimsy, we truly believe!

So gather your threads, let us knot up a tale,
With each little twist, we're destined to fail.
Yet through all the mess, our spirits won't cease,
In this zany adventure, we're stitched up in peace.

The Latch of Loyalty

A door creaks open with a hearty good cheer,
A key full of charm and a dash of sincere.
Each friend a tiny latch that can twist,
To hold tight our secrets, they can't be dismissed.

In the clubhouse of joy, we bounce and we play,
With every small gesture, we brighten the day.
The hinges may rust, but the love stays so new,
A safety of smiles, a bond tried and true.

As we dance round the room, we lift up the floor,
Like pots full of stew, always wishing for more.
But if a few screws get a bit out of place,
We'll laugh till we cry at the funny old face!

So here's to the friends who can unlock the fun,
With laughter as sturdy as rays from the sun.
Though sometimes we wobble and wobble some more,
We bumble together, it's never a bore!

Unraveled Convictions

A thought like a string, it can fray and unwind,
Sometimes all tangled, but joyfully blind.
We hold to our notions like cats hold their tails,
With patience and purrs, we ride out the gales.

A stray idea tosses and juggles the lot,
With giggles and quirks, it's our favorite spot.
The world can be fuzzy, a puzzle to tease,
Yet in this absurdity, we laugh with such ease.

If fabric could speak, oh, the tales it would tell,
Of dreams tied together and wishes that fell.
But when stitches come loose, there's no point in fuss,
We'll patch it with laughter, it's all about trust!

So loosen your grip, let the fancies play free,
With colors so bright, we'll tie them with glee.
For life is a dance with the quirkiest thread,
We're all in this together, with laughter ahead!

Fastened to the Past

Archive of memories, pinned to the wall,
With pictures that giggle, a light hearted sprawl.
Snapshots of moments, some fuzzy, not clear,
Yet each little glance brings a chuckle and cheer.

A button gets lost in the depths of a coat,
An ancient companion that once kept us afloat.
With each little snag, we embrace the delight,
As nostalgia takes flight on this whimsical night.

We gather our trinkets and share with a grin,
A treasure of stories where laughter begins.
A tie that we wore, a joke that they made,
With every old memory, joy's serenade.

So lift up your voice to the ties that we've had,
In a hum of good humor, there's nothing but glad!
This patchwork of moments we cherish with glee,
In the fabric of time, we're forever carefree!

www.ingramcontent.com/pod-product-compliance
Lightning Source LLC
Chambersburg PA
CBHW070309120526
44590CB00017B/2594